Happy Four[th]

Daniel Jacobs

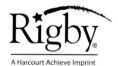

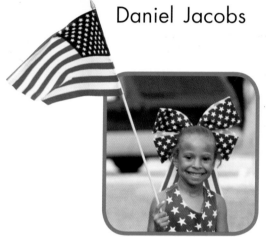

Rigby

A Harcourt Achieve Imprint

www.Rigby.com
1-800-531-5015

We have flags.

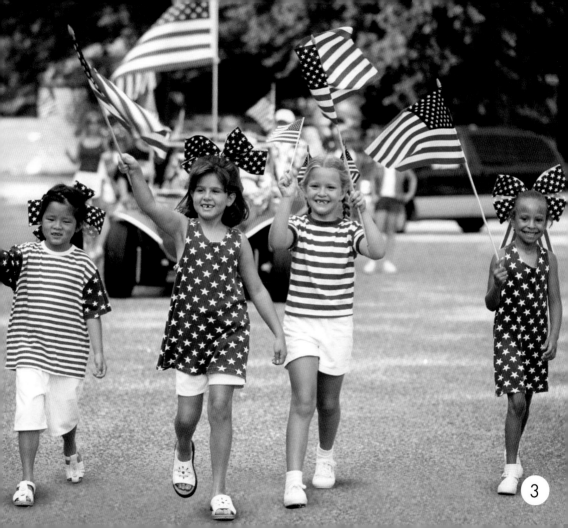

3

We have balloons.

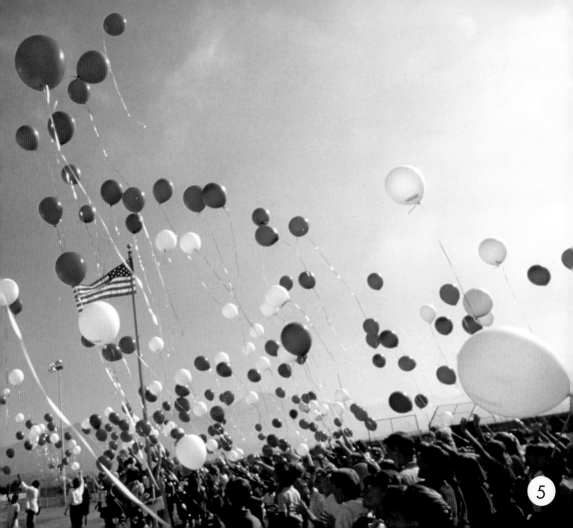

We have stripes!

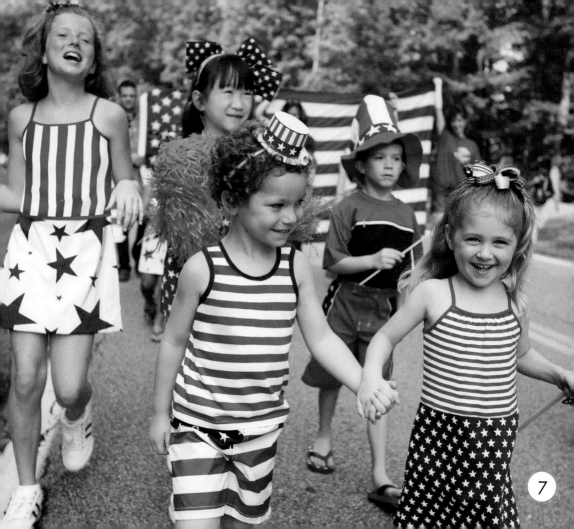

We have parades!

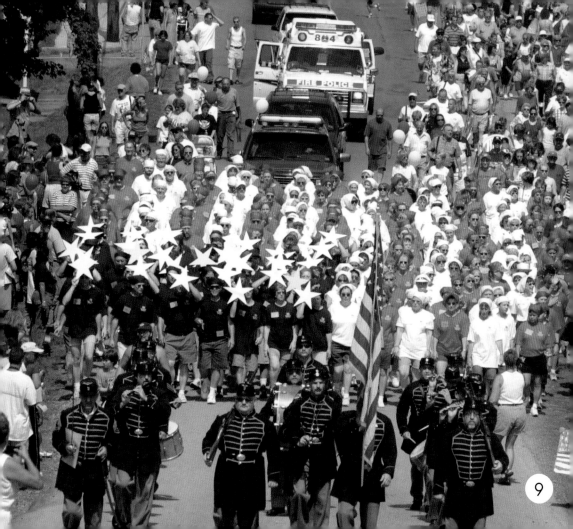

We have food!

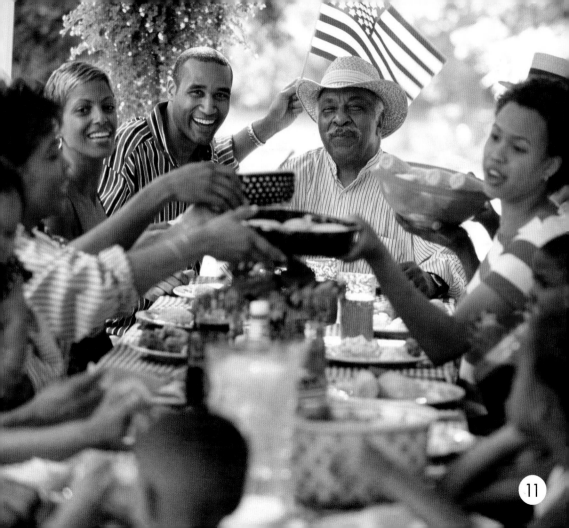

We have games!

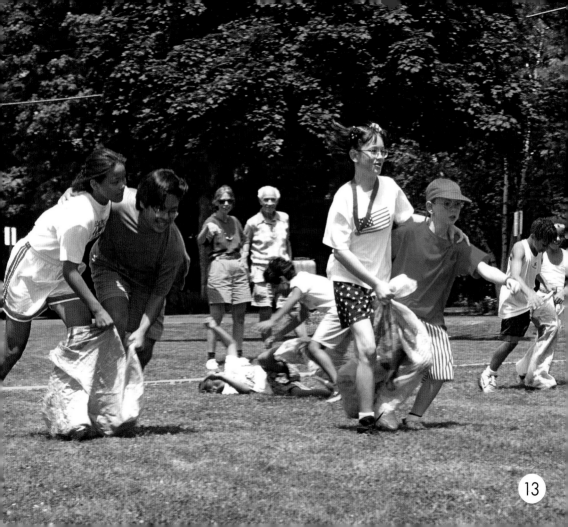

We have fireworks!

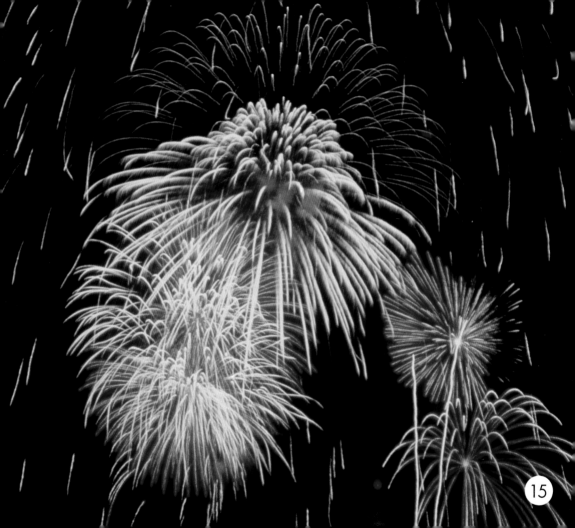

We have fun!

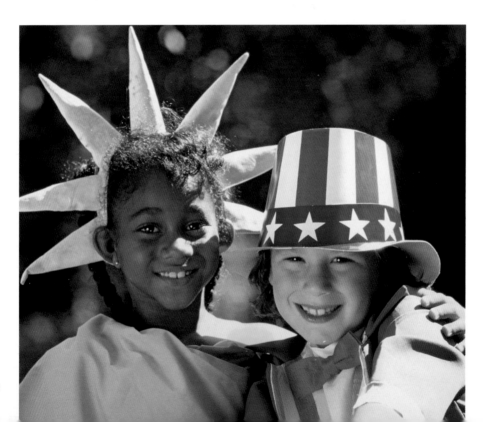